F. S. Burch

ABC Butter making

A hand-book for the beginner

I0191893

F. S. Burch

ABC Butter making
A hand-book for the beginner

ISBN/EAN: 9783743377974

Manufactured in Europe, USA, Canada, Australia, Japa

Cover: Foto ©Andreas Hilbeck / pixelio.de

Manufactured and distributed by brebook publishing software
(www.brebook.com)

F. S. Burch

ABC Butter making

JERSEY COW, MATILDA 4TH.

A B C

BUTTER MAKING

—— A ——

Hand-Book for the Beginner.

BY

F. S. BURCH,

EDITOR OF THE DAIRY WORLD.

~~~~~~~~~~~

CHICAGO:

C. S. BURCH PUBLISHING COMPANY,

1888.

Entered according to Act of Congress, in the year 1888, by

F. S. BURCH,

In the Office of the Librarian of Congress, at Washington, D. C.

CONTENTS.

INDEX TO ILLUSTRATIONS.

PREFACE.

I DO not claim anything new or startling for this little work, nor do I claim to be what is usually termed "an authority" on the subject treated. A B C BUTTER MAKING is the result of my own experience in the dairy, together with an extended and careful observation of the experiences and practices of some of the most successful butter-makers in the country, and is an answer, in a complete form, to the numberless questions asked me (as Editor of the DAIRY WORLD), by beginners in the dairy.

THE AUTHOR.

MILKING.

BEFORE we can make butter we must have milk, and a few suggestions on this important question will not be out of place here. In order that no dirt or hairs may find their way into the milk-pail, a careful dairyman will always brush off the teats and udder of his cow before he begins to milk, yet, I am sorry to say, thousands of men who profess to be careful dairymen do not know this, and are sometimes guilty of that most uncleanly habit of softening up the teats by squeezing out a little milk on their hands. A large number of cows are utterly ruined every year by improper milking; irregular milking spoils a large number; noisy, loud talking and rough milkers help to spoil a good many more. The very slow milker, as well as the quick, jerky milker, who never strips the cow thoroughly, are helping to make a large number of our cows unprofitable. Six o'clock in the morning and six o'clock in the evening are by far the best hours to do the milking.

Some of our deep milkers should be milked
three times a day for a week or more after
calving. I might write a chapter on kicking
cows, but after a wide and exceedingly costly
experience in this line will simply say I do
not believe in them, and would not accept the
best one I ever saw as a gift. I am satisfied
that it is not a good plan to feed or "slop" a
cow during the milking, as a hungry animal
will be too deeply absorbed in eating to "give
down" all the milk. Better feed just before
or immediately after milking. Keep strangers
away from the stable during the milking
hour; never carry on a conversation in a loud
voice with some person in another part of the
stable while milking; in short, do nothing
that will be likely to draw the attention of
your cow, or she will in a greater or less
degree "hold up" a part of the milk. When
possible a cow should always be milked by
the same person, as the milker soon learns
any little peculiarity of the animal, and knows
exactly how to handle her, as well as readily
detecting any unusual occurrence, such as
shortage of milk, sore or caked teats, etc.
Milk as rapidly as possible, without jerking,
and avoid hurting the teats with sharp and
long finger nails by keeping them well pared.
Never attempt to draw the milk from a very

sore or inflamed teat with your hands; it
only causes the animal great pain, and in nine
cases out of ten you will fail to secure all of
the milk. Milking tubes, made of silver, are
not only great conveniences, but now that
they can be bought so cheaply, are an absolute
necessity, and all farmers should keep a few
on hand for use in case of an emergency. The
silver tubes are the best, and can be purchased
for half a dollar each of almost any dealer in

dairy goods. I have mailed thousands of
them during the past few years to dairymen
in all parts of the country, and have received
hundreds of letters stating that valuable
cows have been saved that would otherwise
have been ruined for milking, but for the
use of these tubes. It might be well to say
right here that in no case would I recommend
the use of tubes for regular milking, as their
constant use would soon distend the orifice of
the teat, so that it would leak. Grease or wet
the tubes before inserting, and be careful to
push in slowly. If the teat is very sore the
tubes may be allowed to remain in the teat

for a day or two, but I would advise that they
be removed after each milking when possible,
and always wiped perfectly dry.

A good milking stool not only adds com-
fort to the milker, but helps to facilitate the
work to a greater degree than one would
naturally suppose. I give an illustration of
a handy stool, and as a novice can easily

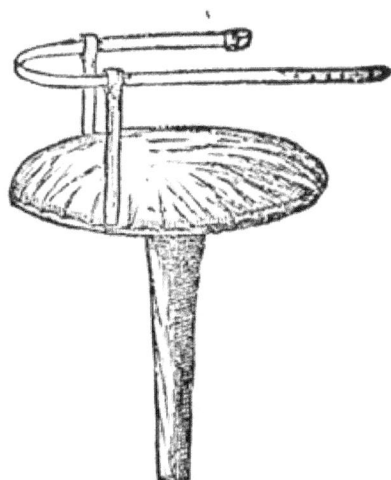

make one, I will simply say, make the leg according to the length of your own. Before
closing this chapter on milking I want to say
a word about the pail. Never use a wooden
pail or vessel to milk in. The best pail I
ever used was a patent device called the
"Michigan Milk Bucket," and were it not for
the expense (I believe the price is two dollars),
they would soon come into general use. The

illustration shows exactly what they are—a
combined pail, strainer and stool ; and as the

strainer prevents any dirt or hairs from get-
ting into the pail, and the close-fitting cover
precludes any possibility of the milk absorb-
ing stable odors, I cannot say too much in
their praise.   When these pails were first
placed on the market the strainer was at the
bottom of the receiving cup, and all the dirt
was washed into the pail, but the manufacturers altered them by placing the strainer an
inch above the bottom of the receiver, and I
believe that they are now as near perfect a
milk-pail as one could ask for.

THE CARE OF MILK.

I SHALL not attempt to enter into the chemistry of the milk. It would be out of place in this A B C treatise. One peculiar thing I wish to draw your attention to is the "animal heat." When the milk first comes from the cow you cannot help noticing that it has a sort of feverish smell, which soon passes off after exposure to the air. This "cowey" smell should, of course, be allowed to pass off, but not in the stable, where the milk would be likely to take on a worse and more lasting odor.

Milk is a great absorbent, and quickly takes on any and all odors which it comes in contact with, and when once taken on, they can never be got rid of. Therefore, the moment we are through milking a cow, we should either take the milk out of the stable and into another room, or pour it at once into a can or some vessel with a tight-fitting cover, that it may not absorb stable odors before we are through with the milking of all the cows. I think the best plan is to strain the milk at once into an ordinary deep setting can and

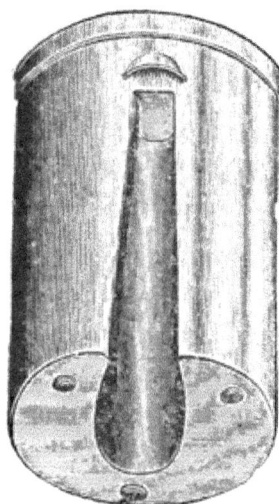

HANEY CAN, BACK VIEW.

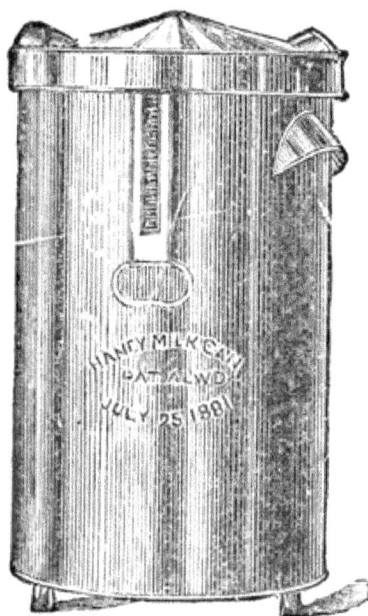

HANEY CAN.

put the cover on tight. Remove the can, as soon as it is filled, to the milk-room.

Now comes the cooling of the milk. To make good butter we must cool our milk rapidly. The sooner we cool it down to 47 degrees after it leaves the cow the better the butter will be. The old-fashioned way of setting the milk in shallow pans or crocks in the milk cupboard, which in summer was placed in the cellar and in the pantry in winter, is still kept up by a good many farmers, and this no doubt accounts for the steady pro-

duction of ten-cent store butter with which
our markets are always overstocked. If you
expect to make good butter never set the
milk in the pantry or cellar, as the odors
which it will absorb there are just as numer-
ous, if not quite so bad, as those in the cow
stable. There is but one way, and dairymen
are pretty generally agreed upon it, and that
is to set the milk in
deep cans in cold
water, and the colder
the water the quicker
the separation of the
cream from the milk.
If you cannot afford
to buy the patent
deep setting cans
like the Cooley, the
Hancy, the Jersey,
or the Wilhelm, by
all means get the
common deep set-
ting "shot - gun"
can, with or without
the glass gauges in

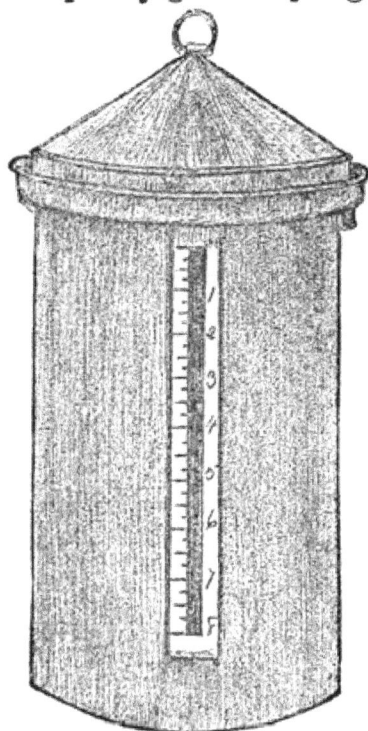

JERSEY CAN.   the sides. The purpose of all these cans is to
cool the milk rapidly, and though the manu-
facturers of this or that can may claim that
their can does the work more quickly than

the others, I am of opinion that they are all good, and one as good as the rest. If you have a spring, and can set the cans in the ground, where the water can flow all around and over the cans, you will be fortunate indeed. If you have no spring, and cannot afford a creamer, make a tank a little deeper

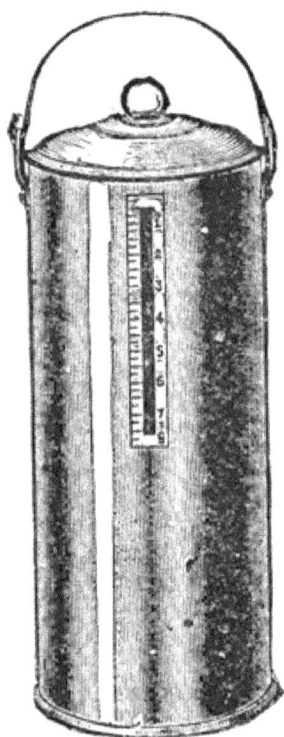

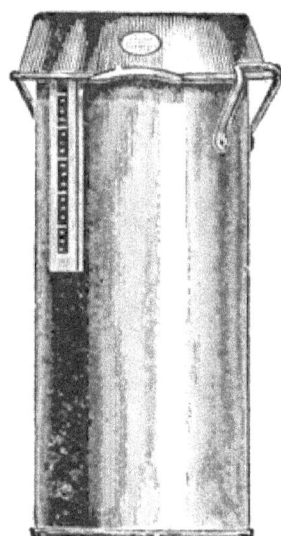

"SHOT-GUN" CAN.   COOLEY CAN.

than the cans, and keep the water flowing around the cans. The colder the water the better. If the water from your well is not colder than 47 degrees you should use ice.

By using ice or very cold spring or well water you get all, or nearly all, the cream to rise in from twelve to twenty hours, and as I said before, and I want to firmly impress it upon your minds, the quicker you get the cream to rise the better butter you can make. Never allow the milk to set more than thirty hours, as it becomes acid or too thick, and loses much in flavor. I would much prefer to skim sooner, if I lost some of the cream by so doing, as I would more than make up what I lost in quantity by the improved quality.

CURTA 4TH (1131)

THE MILK-ROOM.

....

IT would be well to say a word about the milk-room before passing on to the management of cream. It is absolutely necessary that we have a good milk-room in which to not only set the milk, but to ripen the cream, do the churning, and work the butter.

Have the milk-room well ventilated, and build it so that you can control the temperature at the proper point all the year 'round. A good airy place, with plenty of elbow-room is essential. I see too many small, "stuffy" crowded rooms, where there is scarcely a place for half the utensils. Now, see that the air in your room is always pure, and do not pollute it by going directly into it from the cow stable, with all the odors clinging to your clothes and manure on your boots. Also have the room situated as far from the barnyard and hog-pen as possible.

MANAGEMENT OF CREAM.

Skim the milk before the cream becomes too thick and tough on top. I never allow

the cream to remain on the milk a moment
after I think it is all up or separated from
the milk. If you use the deep setting cans
you will find the little conical skimmer, with
ten or twelve inch handle, the easiest to skim
with.

If you put the cream in a can, or other vessel containing cream that was skimmed some
hours previous, be sure to stir it all well
together, so that it may be of the same con-
sistency. Keep the cream at a temperature
of 62 to 68 degrees until it becomes slightly
sour, when it is ready for churning. I have
churned very sweet cream and very sour
cream, but have never been able to get butter
of good flavor from anything but slightly
soured cream. I am also of the opinion that
butter made from cream only slightly sour
will keep much longer than when made from
a very sweet or sour cream. I am often asked
if I think that straining the cream is an ad-
vantage, and I will answer by saying that I
do think it aids somewhat in helping the

butter to come more evenly. In the winter it may be found necessary to place the cream near the stove, where it can be gradually warmed up to 68 or even 70 degrees, in order to have it sufficiently sour.

BUTTER COLOR.

WE all prefer to have our butter of a rich
orange color. White butter looks too
much like lard. Then, too, butter of a pale
white hue never sells for as much in the market as the rich colored article. Years ago
people colored butter with the juice of carrots;
later on the seeds of the Annato plant were

BRANCH OF ANNATO TREE, SHOWING BLOSSOMS
AND SEED PODS.

crushed and the juice mixed with potash and water. We now have many specially prepared compounds in the market, put up in liquid form and ready for immediate use. Almost all of these commercial colors are good, but should be used sparingly. Nearly all the beginners use too much the first time. There is no general rule to follow in using color, and you will only be able to tell how much to use by practice, as the butter of some cows is naturally of a richer color than others ; this is especially true of the Jersey cows, the butter from which needs but little artificial coloring. Always put the coloring into the cream before beginning to churn.

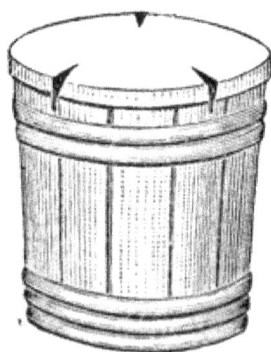

CHURNING.

FEW persons know how to churn properly.
No matter how rich or nice the cream, if
the churning is not done at a proper temperature and in a proper manner you cannot
make good butter. Avoid the "lightning"
patent churn, which the agent will claim to

RECTANGULAR CHURN.

bring butter in five minutes. Cream that
is churned too quickly always makes butter
of a cheesey flavor, and quick to get rancid.

Churning should never be done in less than twenty minutes, and, if possible, not longer than forty minutes. Generally the proper temperature at which to have the cream before beginning to churn is 60 degrees, but sometimes this must be varied a few degrees, according to circumstances. In winter we find 65 or 68 degrees will be necessary in order to have the butter come within forty minutes. When cows are fresh the butter comes much more quickly than it will after they have been fresh for a long period. Always start the

PENDULUM CHURN.

churn with a slow movement, gradually increasing until you have reached the proper speed, which is 40 to 50 strokes per minute.

I do not believe in the churn with a dash inside, nor do I believe in keeping the churn in motion a moment after the cream breaks. All sensible dairymen are trying to keep pace with the times, and have adopted the granular

BOWL OF GRANULAR BUTTER.

plan. This idea of scooping out great lumps of butter from a churn, and trying to squeeze and rub out the buttermilk with its caseous and albuminous matters is a thing of the past. Squeeze and press and knead all you please, and nothing but the water of the buttermilk will come out; the very impurities which you desire to get out of the butter will be all the more firmly incorporated in it. Not one butter-maker in ten (no, nor fifty) knows enough to stop the churn at the proper time, when the butter has formed into little pellets the size of a wheat kernel. When those little pellets have formed, pull out the plug or stopper in the bottom of your churn; if you have not got such a thing as a hole in your churn, don't waste a moment until you have bored one there, at least an inch in diameter, and place a small piece of very fine wire sieve on the inside of the churn over the hole, and thereafter be careful not to have your plug so long that it will punch the sieve off every time you put it in. Let the buttermilk drain off through this hole, after first pouring in a little cold water and cooling the contents of churn down to a point where the globules or kernels of butter will stick together when you agitate the churn. Now let the churn stand and rest a few minutes, then pour in more cold water, and let it drain off through the hole again, and if the water comes out as clear as it went in, stop pouring, shake the churn a little, then make a good strong brine of well powdered salt that has been first sifted thoroughly, cork up the hole and pour in your brine, and let it stand on the butter for fifteen or twenty minutes, after which draw off as you did the water. You now have your butter in the best possible condition for working. When you purchase your churn be sure and get one large enough; it is much better to have it too large than not large enough. If you think you have not sufficient cream

BARREL CHURN.

for a churning and the cream is ripe, do not wait for another skimming, but add sufficient milk to have the churn filled to about one-fourth its capacity. Do not use milk that is very sour, as it is likely to contain so much casein that your butter will not be of good flavor. Many dairymen churn all the milk with the cream, but as it only adds more work to the churning, I do not recommend it except in cases where there is not cream enough to properly fill the churn. Illustrations are given of the best churns for the dairy, viz., the Barrel Churn, the Rectangular Churn, and the Pendulum Churn.

WORKING THE BUTTER.

NEVER work the butter when it is too warm. I find that 56 degrees is about right. The main point in working butter is to get the buttermilk all out, and also to get it in good solid compact form. More depends upon proper working than one would naturally suppose. You often see butter with great

HOME-MADE DANISH BUTTER WORKER.

drops of buttermilk standing all over it; such butter was only half worked, and will generally contain thirty to forty per cent. of water.

and will keep sweet but a very short time.
The other extreme is overworking, and
this produces a dry crumbly mass, with
no flavor. If the churning is done as described in the foregoing chapter very little

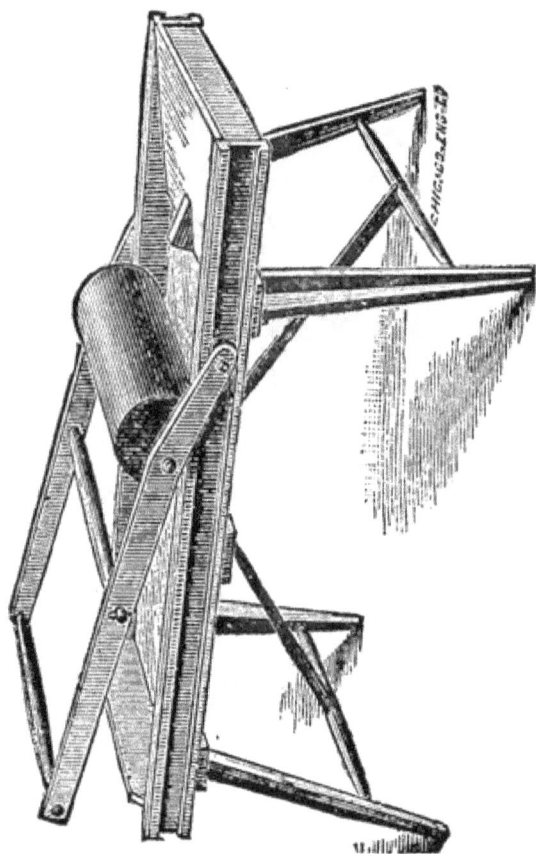

EUREKA BUTTER WORKER.

working is necessary, as the buttermilk is
very nearly all out of the butter before it
leaves the churn. Take the butter out of the
churn with your butter spade, and heap it up

on the worker. If too warm for working at
once, throw a cloth wet in cold water over it,
and leave to drain and cool for thirty minutes.
Before using the lever of your worker always
dip it in cold water. Now take the lever and
gently press the butter out over the full sur-
face of the worker, and sprinkle on some salt;
begin at the sides, and roll the butter back

WATERS' PATENT BUTTER WORKER.

into the centre, being careful not to do any
rubbing or you will have greasy butter. Now
press out the whole mass again, and give it
another salting, and repeat the working two
or three times until you have incorporated
the salt throughout the whole mass evenly.
The general rule for salting is to use one
ounce of salt to a pound of butter, but as
some people like "salty" butter and some
"fresh" butter, you must salt according to
the wants of your patrons. I always use a
fine sieve, and sift the salt over the butter on

the worker, just as the baker sifts his flour over the dough when making it. Much depends upon the quality of the salt used in butter-making, and if you desire to make good

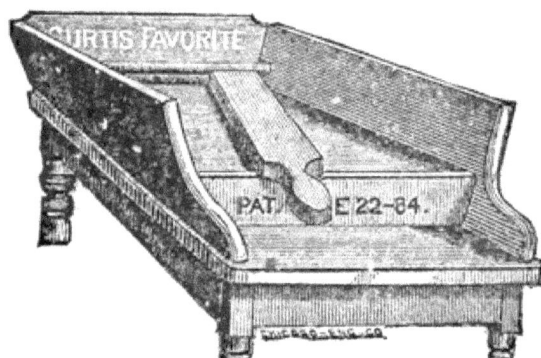

CURTIS FAVORITE BUTTER WORKER, FOR ONE OR TWO COWS.

butter use only good salt, which is put up in sacks, and branded "Dairy Salt," by nearly all the large salt makers in the country. If

BUTTER-SALTING SCALE.

you have a large dairy do not trust to guesswork, but buy a scale and use it. An illustration of a scale which is made especially for salting butter is given above. These scales

weigh from one-half ounce up to 250 pounds,
and as they can be used for ordinary weighing without regard to the butter-salting at-
tachment, every dairyman should have one.
They cost about six dollars.

An illustration of a home-made butter
worker, which is used largely by the Danes, is
herewith given. Any man that is handy
with tools, can make one. Cuts of three
other good workers are shown; they are well
made, and cost but a small amount.

MARKETING BUTTER.

"BUTTER well made is half sold," says an old maxim; but one would naturally suppose that it was "quite sold," to observe the careless manner in which four-fifths of the farmers market their butter. Who has not observed the tactics of the country storekeeper in buying butter? Here comes Mrs. Smith, or Jones, who is known near and far as a good butter maker. See how anxious the merchant is to please her; he knows that her butter is in great demand and will be sold at a good price before night. He pays her the highest market price, and while weighing the neat prints of golden butter, carefully wrapped in spotless cloth or snow-white parchment paper, tells her that he wishes she could have brought in more. It's a pleasure to have the trade of such a woman. But now comes Mrs. Easy. Observe the cloudy expression on the merchant's countenance, as he tells her that he's overstocked with butter; that the market is "way down." You will notice that he charges her a "long

price" for whatever he sells her, and dumps
her butter, which is generally in mussy rolls,
into the nearest shoe box. And who can
blame him, knowing that he cannot sell Mrs.
Easy's butter at home, but must ship it to the
nearest market and sell it for "low grade
dairy" at a price which seldom, if ever, nets
him a profit.

One seldom hears of the markets being
over-stocked with "gilt edge" butter; on the
other hand, the market is nearly always loaded
down with "low grades" and grease.

The best plan for marketing butter is to
endeavor to find customers at home, and sell
as soon as possible. People that pack their
butter and wait f r a rise, are sometimes dis-
appointed, and no butter can be as good four
or six months after it is made as when fresh.
It is far better, as a rule, to sell as soon as
possible, at the best price you can get, than to
wait for a rise that sometimes fails to come.

I receive many letters during the year from
people asking me to find them city customers,
Such customers, as a rule, are very exacting;
they expect much, and paying a high price,
have a perfect right to do so. These private
customers (unless acquainted with the butter
maker) seldom prove agreeable people to deal
with. It is better to sell for a few cents less

at home, and leave no chance for dissatisfaction, or if you cannot possibly sell all you make at home, better ship it to some reliable commission merchant, and leave him to fight out the battle with the customers. A good plan is to make up a sample pail or tub, and ship to the commission merchant with a request that he "judge" and report on it, with any suggestions he has to offer. Such a request will be sure to bring you a prompt report from any good dealer.

PACKING AND SHIPPING.

THE size, shape and style of package for butter makers to use, must depend largely upon the demands of the market to which the butter is shipped. A few years ago large quantities of roll butter were marketed in Chicago during the colder months; now you may travel from one end of the market to the other and not see a hundred rolls. It is but a short time ago that earthen crocks and jars were extensively used; now you scarcely ever see them. The cause for this is, that earthen vessels, of any kind, are not only liable to break, but are also more difficult to handle in large quantities, and weigh much more than wooden packages. The great bulk of butter that comes to Chicago now, is packed

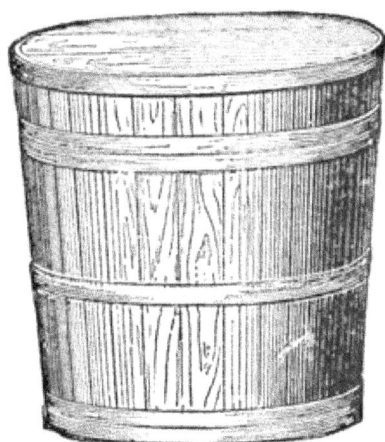

WHITE ASH BUTTER TUB

in white ash tubs and bale boxes. Occasionally we see a tin package with wood veneer, but they have never come into general use for the reason that the acid gets under the tin and causes rust. Wooden packages are just now most popular, and as the manufacturers have reduced the cost of manufacturing them to a point where earthenware and tin cannot compete in price, we may look to see them in use for years to come. The ordinary white ash tubs can be had of every dairy supply dealer and nearly all of the general stores; they may be had in 20 lb., 25 lb., 30 lb., 40 lb. and 60 lb. sizes. An illustration of the nine-pound bale boxes in crate is also given. During the last two years

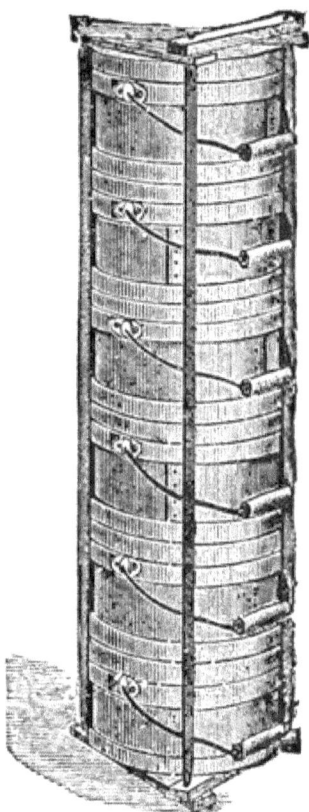

NINE POUND BALE
BOXES.

these bale boxes have become very popular. They can be shipped in crates of six and are convenient to handle; they can be had for about twelve cents apiece.

In packing butter in wooden vessels we
must guard against "woody taste," and there
is but one way to do this, that is, to soak the
packages from 24 to 48 hours in strong brine
and then thoroughly scald them out.   Even
this method sometimes fails to accomplish the
work.   A capital way to prevent woody taste,
is to line the package with parchment paper,
which not only prevents the butter from tak-
ing on a woody flavor, but also prevents soak-
age and excludes the air.   This parchment
paper may now be had of all dairy implement
dealers, in sheets and circles of any size.   It
costs about thirty cents a pound, and a pound
is sufficient to pack several hundred pounds
of butter.

There is still quite a trade in print butter,
and when nicely packed in one or two-pound
prints and of good quality it sells quickly, on
account of its convenient shape for family
use.   For print butter there has been invented
a machine which stamps out one-half and one-
pound blocks very quickly and quite artistically.   When butter is shipped in this form
it should be first carefully wrapped in cloth
or parchment paper and packed in boxes in
crates.   Each box should contain but one
block of butter, as piling one block upon
another would be likely to press out the deli-

cate figures moulded or stamped on the block.
The blocks for these patent printing machines
are sometimes artistically carved, so that the
blocks of butter show sheaves of wheat, acorns,
etc., and sometimes with the maker's initials
or monogram. For home use the old fashioned round mould holding from a quarter of

I X L BUTTER PRINTER.

a pound to two pounds is still extensively
used, and when properly soaked in cold water
before moulding, makes a very nice print of
butter. These patent printers and moulds
save much time and are a great convenience
over the old way of forming the butter into
rolls.

In packing it is always better to pack each churning in a separate tub or box, as the tub that contains different churnings will not be of uniform solidity or color throughout, and

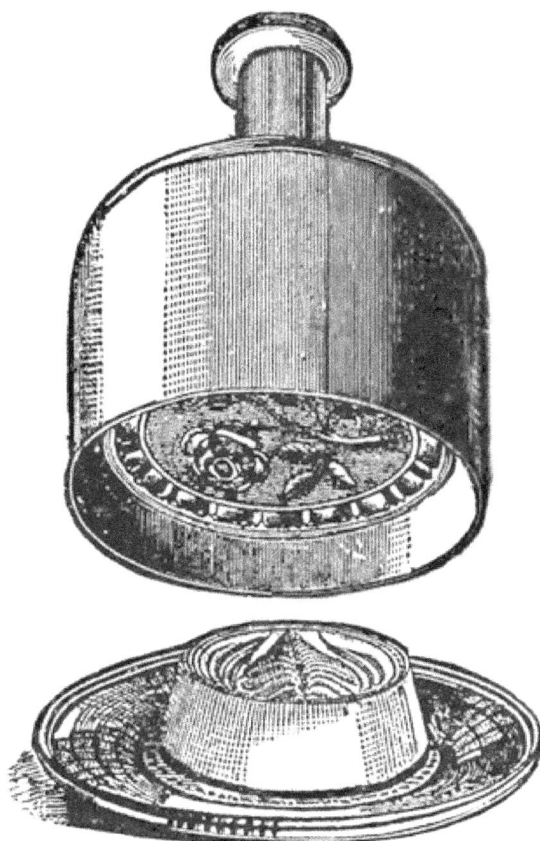

ONE POUND BUTTER MOULD.

will therefore not sell for as much as a tub perfectly uniform.

Remember to soak the covers of the packages, and before fastening them on sprinkle salt to a depth of a quarter of an inch over the top of the butter cloth or paper. Never leave the cover off the packages for any length of time, for the reason that it will not only cause the top of the butter to become discolored, but it will also admit the air and spoil the top of the butter for several inches.

The moment you have packed your butter get it into a cool place—the cooler the better —and thereafter keep it as cool as possible, until you have disposed of it.

THERMOMETERS IN THE DAIRY.

FREDERIC SUMNER says "There is no more use in trying to run a dairy without a good tested thermometer than there would be to attempt sailing a vessel without a rudder," and I heartily agree with him. A good thermometer can be purchased for from fifty cents to a dollar, and at these prices is certainly within the reach of every dairyman. Too much depends upon the temperature of the water in which we cool our milk, the room we ripen our cream in, do our churning in, and the temperature of the milk, cream, and the butter itself, to attempt any guess work. Our grandmothers used thumb and finger to ascertain the temperature of milk and cream, but in these days of fifty cents, seventy-five cents, and a dollar a pound butter we find "thumb-rule" will not work. An illustration

of a thermometer made expressly for dairy use, is given ; they are made of glass and float upright in the milk or cream. The churning and cheese points are marked for the convenience of new beginners ; they retail at about fifty cents, and can be purchased from any dealer in dairy goods.

MAXIMS

For A B C Butter Makers.

TEST your cows.

Never fill the churn over half full.

Never touch the butter with your hands.

Cream rises best in a falling temperature.

Never churn fresh unripened cream with ripened cream.

After cream becomes sour, the more ripening the more it depreciates.

The best time for churning is just before the acidity becomes apparent.

Never let your butter get warm ; when once warmed through it will lose its flavor.

Excessive working makes crumbly butter, spoils the grain and injures the flavor.

Never mix night's with morning's milk, as the warmth of the new and the coldness of the old, hastens change and decomposition.

All kinds of disagreeable odors are easily absorbed by salt. Keep it, therefore, in a clean, dry place, in linen sacks, if it is to be used for butter making.

The best butter has the least competition to contend against, while the worst dairy products have the most. The better anything is, the more rare is it and the greater its value.

A butter maker that uses his fingers instead of a thermometer, to find out the temperature of milk or cream will never make a success.

Cleanliness should be the Alpha and Omega of butter making. Absolute cleanliness as regards person, stable, utensils and package.

Faults—The quickest way to find out the faulty points in your butter, is to send a sample of it to some reliable butter buyer and ask him to score it.

The difference between the dairyman who makes $50.00 a year, per cow, and one who makes $30.00, is that the first works intelligently, the second mechanically.

Details—The price of success in butter making, as in all other classes of business, is strict attention to the little details; it's the sum of all these little things that determines whether your butter is to be sold for ten cents a pound or as a high priced luxury.

The disadvantages of the system of setting milk in shallow pans or crocks, for raising cream, are that a long period elapses before the skimming is completed, too much space is required, and in Summer the milk becomes sour before the whole of the cream is raised.

Labor saving appliances are intended, as
the name implies, to save labor, but they do
not render care, thought and diligence the
less necessary. To understand the principles
that underlie the business of butter making,
is as imperative as to use the most improved
utensils.

By keeping a strict account only, can you
find out the extent of your success or failure.
If the balance is on the right side, you will
know whether and how much it can be in-
creased; if it is on the wrong side, you will
be more strongly convinced of the necessity
for improvement.

If you keep your cows in a healthy condition, milk regularly; set the milk in air tight
cans with good cold water (either ice or
spring); skim every twenty-four hours; ripen
the cream properly; churn in a barrel churn
or some other good churn on the same prin-
ciple; wash the butter well while still in the
churn in granular state; you will never be
troubled with white specks in your butter.

HOW TO MAKE GOOD BUTTER.

—BY N. BIGALOW, STOWE, VERMONT.—

IT is necessary to have good cows to start with, and if *good butter* is the object sought I prefer good Jerseys. The next thing is good feed. Grass that is fresh and tender is best of all. This does not last very long up here in Vermont. My cows have a feed of green corn fodder, at night, and a small feed of grain, in the morning. I prefer to mix different kinds of grain together. It must be all sound and good. Make the cows comfortable and contented. Kind treatment is indispensable, and the more regularity in caring for them the better.

We try to keep the milk entirely clean. If it is necessary we wash the cows' bags, before milking. The milk is strained into large, open pans, and as soon as the animal heat is out of it, the pans are covered over with thin cotton cloth. The covers are made by sewing the edges of the cloth to some strips of basswood, about three-fourths of an inch square and a little longer than the pans. They cost but a trifle, and after using them ten years we would hardly make butter without them. The butter is not quite so yellow, at first, for raising the cream under the covers, but will be after it has stood a few hours.

When we first tried our large pans, we used to run water around them, but the coolers have got to leaking, and we do not think it would pay to get new ones.

Our rule is to skim the milk soon after it sours, as the cream will come off easily. We keep the cream in a cellar, when it is necessary, but prefer to keep it in the milk room, when it is not too warm. Our dairy is small, and we have churned only twice a week, this year. We use the Stoddard churn, and would not use a float churn. I have never seen the acme churn yet, and hardly think it has been made. 58 degrees is the right temperature at which to churn the cream, in warm weather: 62 in cold, and 60 in spring and fall. We put in from three to six quarts of water to thin the cream, and if the cream is too warm we use cold water (we have a cold spring), and in extreme warm weather use a little ice. If the cream is too cold we warm the water sometimes up to 120 degrees. If that will not answer, the cream

must be warmed beforehand. The buttermilk is drawn off as soon as it can be done,
and leave most of the butter in the churn.
Any butter that runs out is put back with a
skimmer. We use cold water enough to keep
the butter in the grain, and wash it until the
water runs clear. I suppose brine would be
better, but have not used it much. After the
butter has drained, the salt is strained in with
a paddle; and then it is taken out with the
paddle and pressed into the butter bowl. We
use about an ounce of salt to a pound, but
some of it works out. After it has stood a
few hours, it is worked with a lever in an old
fashioned butter worker, just enough to get
the salt in evenly, and then it is ready to
print. We always try to injure the grain as
little as possible.

Our printer holds four pounds, and makes
eight half pound prints. The prints are put
up in four pound boxes, and cut apart with
wooden blades. The boxes are made here in
Stowe, and are washed and scalded with boil-
ing water, sprinkled with salt.

Our milk house is shaded on the eastern
side by a willow tree, and on the southern by
another building, and we can cool it to some
extent with currents of air. But if we should
admit currents of air, without the covers over

the pans, there would be white specks in the butter.

We use butter color when it is necessry to color the butter, but think it better to color it too little than too much.

I am in the habit of mixing a small quantity of cotton seed meal with the grain for the cows, and think I get a little more milk from that than anything else. Linseed meal is very high here, and I have never used it.

Last, but not least, the cows must have pure air to breathe, and the milk, cream and butter must be kept in a good atmosphere.

I am fully convinced that any farmer that makes a prime article of butter, of uniform quality, has an excellent opportunity to use common sense and sound judgment.

Consumers of such butter, as I have described, need not have any fear that they are eating anything that is, or *ever was*, filthy or unwholesome.

www.ingramcontent.com/pod-product-compliance
Lightning Source LLC
Chambersburg PA
CBHW032033090426
42733CB00031B/820